KNOWLEDGE ENCYCLOPEDIA
INVERTEBRATES

© Wonder House Books 2022

All rights reserved. No part of this book may be reproduced or transmitted in any form by any means, electronic or mechanical, including photocopying and recording, or by any information storage and retrieval system except as may be expressly permitted in writing by the publisher.

(An imprint of Prakash Books)

contact@wonderhousebooks.com

Disclaimer: The information contained in this encyclopedia has been collated with inputs from subject experts. All information contained herein is true to the best of the Publisher's knowledge.

ISBN : 9789354400247

Table of Contents

Spineless Wonders	3
Evolution of Invertebrates	4–5
Tough Invertebrates	6–7
The Invertebrate Family	8–9
Chemical Warfare	10
Migratory Invertebrates	11
Clever Camouflage	12
Hearty Meals	13
The Ancient Sponges	14–15
The Colourful Corals	16–17
Parasitic Invertebrates	18–19
The Slimy Snails	20–21
Meet the Squids	22–23
The Friendly Earthworms	24
The Bloodthirsty Leeches	25
Crabs & Other Crustaceans	26–27
Creepy Crawlies	28–29
Star of the Show	30–31
Word Check	32

SPINELESS WONDERS

The term 'invertebrate' refers to living organisms without any vertebrae or backbone. All invertebrates lack backbones. These are amongst the oldest forms of living organisms, having evolved millions of years before the first vertebrates—the fish. But this life form still survives!

In fact, invertebrates not only survive, they thrive. Invertebrates account for almost 97 per cent of animals on Earth. Diversity, varied reproductive methods and adaptability have made them one of the most resilient creatures on this planet. They are found everywhere, like on frozen lands, in hot deserts and deep in the oceans. Turn the page to read about the amazing lives of invertebrates!

▼ *The sea sponge is a perfect example of an invertebrate*

Evolution of Invertebrates

The story of Earth began 4.5 billion years ago. That is a time beyond imagination. The planet was not as we see it today. It was uninhabitable due to high temperatures, volcanic eruptions and collisions with other objects from the newly formed solar system. As time passed by, the planet stabilised. In the course of events, it gave rise to life.

First Life Forms

The first definite fossil evidence of life dates back to 3.5 billion years ago. Life originated in an atmosphere rich in methane and carbon dioxide, but very little oxygen. The first forms were **single-celled bacteria**. Fast forward to 2.5 billion years ago and a new type of bacteria evolved called the cyanobacteria. It was unique as it produced oxygen through a process known as **photosynthesis**.

▶ Stromatolites are fossils of photosynthetic bacteria found in ancient rocks

▲ The chlorophyll-rich cyanobacteria coat the river with green colour. These are tough creatures, still surviving on Earth in large numbers

Snowball Earth

Photosynthesising bacteria flourished and created more and more oxygen. This changed the atmosphere, making it rich in oxygen; while most of the earlier bacteria that depended on methane died out. Then, around 715–660 million years ago, Earth cooled down to such an extent that the temperatures at the equator dropped down to −20° C. This event is called 'Snowball Earth' and is thought to have been triggered by the rapid weathering of continents, which sucked out atmospheric carbon dioxide. Life could not sustain on this snowball. It was wiped out, except near deep-sea volcanic vents.

Cambrian Explosion

About 560 million years ago, the conditions changed and the environment became more habitable—a warm Earth, rising sea levels and of course, generous oxygen levels (a result of the cyanobacteria), lead to the creation of many new life forms. This time period is called the Cambrian Explosion. It was here that the first invertebrates appeared on Earth.

Trilobites

Trilobites are the icons of the Cambrian seas. As the name suggests, trilobites had three segments. They had tough, plated bodies to protect themselves from predators in the seas, and could grow as much as two feet in length. More than 17,000 species survived for millions of years, only to be wiped out at the end of the Permian Period, 251 million years ago. A few of these species were predators and some were scavengers. Many of them ate plankton. All trilobites had antennae and legs.

▲ Trilobites are among the most prolific fossils found in the seas

Isn't It Amazing!

Opabinia, belonging to an extinct group of animals called *Opabinia regalis*, swam the Cambrian seas. This creature had five eyes and caught its prey with a flexible claw-like arm that jutted out of its head. It stayed close to the seafloor, hunting ancient sponges for food.

▲ A fossil specimen of the ancient invertebrate Opabinia regalis

Ancient Creatures

Following the Cambrian explosion, the seas were flooded with a variety of marine invertebrates along with trilobites. These were the graptolites, brachiopods, echinoderms, molluscs, corals and cephalopods. Many of these invertebrates were strange creatures. For example, the orthocone, a tailless, finless animal, was shaped like a long ice-cream cone with tentacles. This 11-metre-long animal cut through waters hunting for prey such as the early species of fish and sea scorpions.

▲ A creature called Cameroceras had a unique shape which helped it jet-propel through the waters

Graptolites

Graptolites lived in colonies. They had tentacles and a **chitinous** outer covering. Most of these animals have been preserved as carbon impressions on shale, a type of a sedimentary rock.

▶ A colony of graptolites that looked like floating umbrellas in the ancient sea

The Pterygotus

Pterygotus, a distant relative of the modern horseshoe crab, was a giant sea scorpion with some species measuring the length of almost eight feet. They were fearsome predators, holding onto their prey, such as early vertebrates as well as other sea dwellers, with their huge pincers. Apart from the pterygotus, almost 200 species of these extinct invertebrates have been identified. The fossils of these animals have been found in brackish and fresh water.

▲ An artist's impression of the pterygotus

Devonian Period

Plants evolved much earlier than first thought by scientists. By the Devonian Period, which was about 416 million years ago, terrestrial vegetation started to spread. These plants did not have roots and shoots. They did not grow more than a few centimetres tall. Dwelling amongst these early plants were mainly arthropods in the form of insects, mites and **myriapods**. Yes, the first insects had already evolved a few million years before the Devonian Period began. The early insects were small, wingless and had simple antennae.

The shallow waters of the Devonian Period saw the development of large coral reefs. The seas continued to be populated by early invertebrates. However, by the end of the Devonian Period, most trilobite species had disappeared.

Passage of Time

Many large invertebrates like the *Arthropleura* grew to their size because there was more oxygen in the environment and fewer vertebrate predators on land. Eventually, these giant invertebrates reduced in size and modern arthropods came into being. It is their adaptability to the changing environment that has made invertebrates a lasting group of animals on this planet. These wonderful creatures were there before us and, according to scientists, will remain even after human beings have disappeared from Earth.

Carboniferous Period

About 360 million years ago during the Carboniferous Period, because of the growth of vast swamp forests, there was a tremendous rise in the levels of oxygen in the atmosphere. This rich oxygen-fed air allowed the arthropods to grow to humungous sizes. An example of this is the *Arthropleura*, a terrestrial organism resembling the modern millipede. It grew to almost 2 metres in length and close to 46 centimetres in width. One of its species is considered to be the largest terrestrial invertebrate ever.

▲ The body of the Arthropleura had 30 segments like many modern millipedes

Tough Invertebrates

According to theories, invertebrates should have been the weakest of all organisms living on Earth. They lack backbones, only a few amongst them have a proper digestive system and many, such as sponges, do not even have brains and the associated intelligence. But in reality, invertebrates are among the toughest organisms on the planet. Read on to find out why it is so.

Unchanged Invertebrates

In the course of evolution, some species of invertebrates have remained unchanged for millions of years and are surviving happily. These are the dragonflies and horseshoe crabs. However, fruit flies are still undergoing evolution. These flies are known to make simple changes in their genetic make-up over time. These changes help them survive changing environments.

▲ Fruit flies have adapted to survive over time

▲ The horseshoe crab has resisted evolution. They are seen on seashores. If the coming waves flip them over, they use their long tails to right themselves

Evolution of Resistance

The evolution of resistant, encapsulated dormant forms of invertebrates has enabled many among their species to survive in extreme conditions. For example, the eggs of freshwater fairy shrimp can remain dormant for months in dried mud, hatching only when the mud is submerged in the water again. These eggs are so resistant that even when exposed to temperatures as high as 99° C and as low as –190° C in laboratories, they have remained completely viable.

Breathing Methods

Earthworms need oxygen for survival, akin to human beings, but they have no lungs to gulp in air like human beings. That is why they breathe through their moist skin. But how do they maintain this moist skin? Not only do they live in damp soil, but also their skin is covered with a thin cuticle and slimy mucus.

Some spiders and scorpions have an interesting apparatus through which they breathe. They are called book lungs, which are a series of membranes that resemble the pages of a book. In between these membranes are air sacs which allow the air to circulate. Aiding the breathing process is the haemolymph, which is similar to the blood of human beings. For many insects, the trachea is the most important respiratory organ. This is usually made up of branching tubes. The trachea sends oxygen to all the tissues in the insect's body and takes away the carbon dioxide. The trachea is modified in insects that have to spend some time underwater. This allows them to exchange gases while they are underwater. These insects are called bubble breathers and the water beetle is the best example.

▲ Fairy shrimp have egg sacs near their tails

Isn't It Amazing!

Haemolymph consists of necessary nutrients which help the organism survive, but insects lack red blood cells as well as haemoglobin, giving haemolymph an almost colourless appearance.

Comb Jelly

The freely swimming comb jelly maintains its spherical shape through the presence of water in the internal canals. These canals support eight rows of comb plates, with which the comb jelly swims. Each comb plate is covered with hair-like cilia which propel the organism forward. The organism swims mouth-first.

▶ *This picture shows an artist's impression of comb jelly*

Structure

The stony coral polyp obtains support from a mineralised theca or a cup which is secreted by the animal. This helps anchor it to the basal structure of the coral colony as well as to its neighbours.

The closely related sea anemone does not use a rigid structure like the stone coral. Instead, it supports itself by using the water circulating around its central cavity. The water is drawn in through grooves on the sides of the cavity and expelled up the centre. It helps the organism maintain shape and internal pressure.

▼ *Hermit crabs have asymmetrical bodies that curl towards their right side*

Protective Armour

Invertebrates that are arthropods or joint-legged animals, such as scorpions, crabs, lobsters and spiders have hard, chitinous, water-resistant exoskeletons which protect them from dehydration and various environmental changes such as extreme heat or heavy rains, as well as predators. This exoskeleton is moulted regularly by the invertebrate; it is while the exoskeleton is growing back that the invertebrate, with its exposed softness, is most vulnerable.

Molluscs such as snails have developed shells for protection, while hermit crabs live in discarded sea shells that wash up the shore, moving to a bigger one as they grow. But what is interesting is that this crab always finds an empty shell; it never kills or throws out the occupants of the shell.

Symmetry

Symmetry is the proportionality or evenness that is displayed on animal bodies. Most invertebrates are divided into three types of symmetries, namely bilateral symmetry, radial symmetry and asymmetry. In bilateral symmetry, the body is divided into two equal parts by an imaginary line. Beetles, crabs and lobsters have bilateral symmetry. In the case of radial symmetry, the body is oriented in a way that an imaginary line radiates through its centre, like in animals such as jellyfish and starfish. Asymmetrical organisms, such as sponges, are those with no symmetry; the body parts in such organisms do not correspond with each other to create a defined shape.

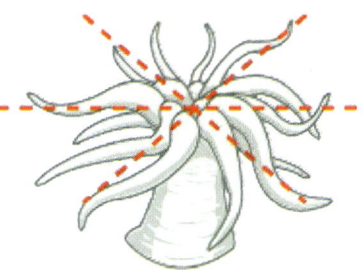
▲ *A coral polyp has radial symmetry*

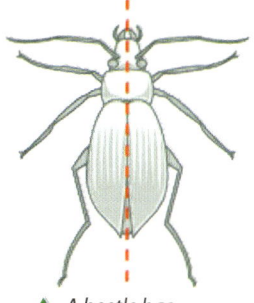
▲ *A beetle has bilateral symmetry*

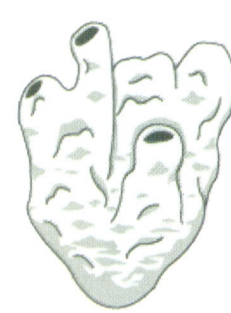
▲ *A sponge has no symmetry*

The Invertebrate Family

Jean-Baptiste Lamarck was a French biologist who coined the term 'invertebrates'. Under this category, he put together all animals that lack the spinal cord. Invertebrates as a group include not just simple life forms such as sponges, but also the complex arthropods. There are more than 30 phyla or groups into which invertebrates are categorised. The major phyla are listed below. Insects, arachnids, molluscs, crustaceans and their species belong to the group of invertebrates. They include animals that live on land and water.

01 Phylum: Porifera

Characteristics: Primitive; asymmetrical; filter out water for food particles; have no tissues but have specialised cells

▲ Sponges

03 Phylum: Platyhelminthes

Characteristics: Aquatic and terrestrial habitats; soft-bodied; bilateral symmetry; incomplete digestive system; have a single opening to take in food and expel waste; **cephalisation**

▶ Fluke

▲ Flatworm

02 Phylum: Cnidaria

Characteristics: Aquatic; free-swimming life forms with radial symmetry; presence of tissues, incomplete digestive system

▶ Jellyfish

▼ Corals

04 Phylum: Nematoda

Characteristics: Aquatic and terrestrial habitats; bilateral symmetry; complete digestive system; have an excretory tube to remove waste

▶ Roundworms

In Real Life

Do you know what a body cavity is? It is a fluid-filled space not referring to blood or lymph vessels. Human beings have several body cavities. Flatworms have a gut, but no other body cavities. There are several smaller invertebrates that do not have any body cavity. As a result, the gut in bigger flatworms sends food to all body parts and makes their body shape flat. They also do not have an anus, which is used to remove waste. Flatworms can be free-living or parasitic. They are the largest phylum of the acoelomates, having nearly 25,000 species within the phylum.

ANIMALS | INVERTEBRATES

05 Phylum: Molluscs

Characteristics: Aquatic and terrestrial habitats; have an organ system; body has a head, a foot and a **visceral** mass; have a true **coelom** and soft bodies which are at times covered with a hard exoskeleton; few have a primitive brain

▲ Octopus ◀ Snail ▼ Squid ▲ Clams

06 Phylum: Annelida

Characteristics: Aquatic and terrestrial habitats; segmented bodies; coelomates; have a primitive brain

▲ Earthworms ▼ Leech ▲ Marine worm

07 Phylum: Echinodermata

Characteristics: Have an organ system with a complete digestive system and brain; presence of a spiny external covering as well as an internal skeleton; most have a **pentamerous** radial symmetry

▶ Sea star ▲ Sea dollars ◀ Sea cucumbers ▲ Sea urchins

Incredible Individuals

While Charles Darwin is credited with the theory of evolution, the idea behind this theory developed well before him in the 1700s. Jean-Baptiste Lamarck also put forth a theory of evolution of his own. He was a botanist who later became an expert on invertebrates and other boneless animals. In his research, he also realised that several animals shared similarities. He confirmed this observation by studying fossil records. He realised that as the environment changed, animals adapted to survive. He used the giraffe as an example of the same. He proposed that giraffes might have developed longer necks and front limbs as a result of a sustained habit of stretching to reach higher leaves on trees.

08 Phylum: Arthropoda

Characteristics: Bilateral symmetry; body divided into head; abdomen and **thorax**; chitinous exoskeleton; joint appendages; presence of a proper brain compared to earlier phyla

▲ Shrimps ▲ Crab ▲ Centipede ▲ Barnacles

Secret for Success

Invertebrates might have everything else going against them, but the big secret behind their successful life and evolution is their rate of reproduction. Some invertebrates like sponges can produce eggs and sperm themselves. Some other invertebrates do not need their eggs to undergo fertilisation; these include ants and bees. Invertebrates, especially insects, adapt easily.

Chemical Warfare

Invertebrates have one of the best chemical defences in the animal world. They use an array of these defences, ranging from jets of boiling caustic fluids, paralysing toxins, and foul-smelling liquids to potent poisons that can cause immense harm. Chemical defence is commonly accompanied by a distinctive colouration or behavioural pattern that serves as a warning to the predators.

Borrowed Threads

Sea slugs lack any form of armour like shells, claws or spines, but they are rarely bothered by even the hungriest of fish. The secret lies in the projections that cover their bodies. Many of these projections contain cnidocytes or stinging cells, which give off a barbed, poison-tipped thread the moment anything touches them.

Sea slugs themselves do not produce this poison. They retain it from their prey, the sea anemone. When sea slugs eat the sea anemones, the stinging cells from the latter's tentacles are not digested. These are transported by the slugs to the projections on their bodies and stored to be used in defence.

▲ *The bright colours of a sea slug serve as the first warning to its predators*

Velvety Smarts

Onychophorans, also known as velvet worms, live in tropical regions. These are known to squirt an odourless fluid from the glands on the ends of the projections on their heads. It can be squirted from a distance of almost 15 centimetres. The fluid then hardens immediately, entangling the predator.

◀ *Though onychophorans look like caterpillars, the two should not be confused*

Whiplash

A whip scorpion raises its abdomen when it senses danger, and releases an acidic spray on its predator, which it dispels from its large glands.

◀ *Whip scorpions do not have tails. They resemble spiders*

Boxy Defence

Box jellyfish are named so because of the box-like appearance of their heads. These are transparent blue in colour. The poison of the box jellyfish is considered to be one of the deadliest in nature. It affects the heart, nervous system as well as skin. It is fatal not just to animals but to human beings as well. If attacked, the victim undergoes intense pain and could die of heart failure. If the victim does survive, the pain can last for months.

▶ *The venom released by the box jellyfish can even stun its prey*

ANIMALS | INVERTEBRATES | 11

Migratory Invertebrates

Marine invertebrates either migrate voluntarily or are swept away by strong ocean currents. Migration is the seasonal movement that relocates the invertebrates from one location to another for reasons including weather, food and reproduction. Invertebrates end up covering a large distance during this time.

Planktonic Organisms

Planktons become aquatic drifters as they are carried forward by ocean currents. They travel vertically in a fixed rhythm. During the night, microscopic planktonic organisms travel in the upper waters and are followed by their predators—the fish. They are also relocated by pelagic birds who live in the open sea and prey on plankton and other plants. Planktons usually remain embedded in the bottom of the ocean during the day and come out at dusk.

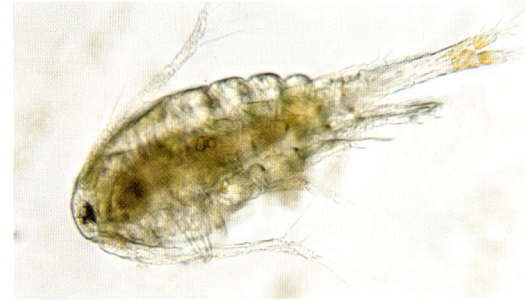

▲ *Freshwater aquatic zooplankton rely on ocean currents to migrate*

Crustaceans

Crustaceans migrate the farthest, especially during their reproductive cycle. Some travel even as far as 240 kilometres! Female crabs, for instance, mate and lay their eggs on the shore before returning to the depths of the ocean.

Some crabs have adapted to land and migrate to the water for the purpose of reproduction. The robber crabs are a classic example of this phenomenon as they return to land right after they finish laying their eggs and are followed back by their young after they have hatched.

The Chinese crabs, among other freshwater crabs, remain in the water for 4–5 years, migrating to brackish waters solely to lay eggs. Their young spend a year in these waters, before migrating back to fresh water.

▲ *Crabs are the most common examples of crustaceans. They are seen on sandy beaches*

Isn't It Amazing!

There are more than 45,000 species of crustaceans that live in different coastal environments. Among them are the amazing crabs which can live in salt water, fresh water and even brackish waters. There are land crabs and sea crabs. But even land crabs need to spend some time in the water. In the water, crabs breathe with their gills which are in cavities under the sides of the carapace. In land crabs, these cavities are much larger and modified to act as lungs.

Seasonal Migration

In the winter, clam worms live among algae and rock crevices. In the summer, they become planktonic and migrate a far distance from the coastal waters in Europe. There, they carry out the process of reproduction. Near Fiji and the South Pacific, the palolo worms develop reproductive cells in the posterior segments. In the months of October and November, the worms live among coral reefs until they shed off their genital cells and rise to the surface of the waters.

▶ *The painted crayfish is a benthic species. It lives and even migrates across the bottom of the ocean*

Clever Camouflage

Camouflage means to blend in the surroundings. Invertebrates use different methods of camouflage while waiting for a prey or while hiding from a predator. Many animals have been using this tactic for millions of years. They are impressive in their array of colours and patterns. Invertebrates might be tough, and they may possess chemical weapons, but in the big bad world, being small creatures, many need to use camouflage to survive.

The Sandy Ghost

Ghost crabs blend well in the sand dunes that are available in plenty on the beaches that they inhabit. The word 'ghost' in their name refers to the fact that these crabs can quickly disappear from sight using their six strong legs. They use camouflage well and lie in wait on the beach, with just two eyes protruding out. The moment prey such as other crabs, lizards, insects or clams, approaches them, the ghost crabs grab and devour it. To hide from the predator, ghost crabs simply vanish into their small burrows.

▲ Ghost crabs are also known as sand crabs

Light Play

Cuttlefish belong to the mollusc family. They have eight arms and two tentacles which are used to capture the prey. The cuttlefish have the amazing ability to change colour within seconds. They do it with the help of pigmented organs called chromatophores. The invertebrate expands or contracts these chromatophores, creating an array of colours. The colour-changing property of the cuttlefish is one of the best camouflage techniques on the planet.

▲ Cuttlefish have venom which can be deadly for human beings if consumed

Deadly Golden Touch

The goldenrod crab spider, or flower spider, can blend in with a range of flowers by changing its colour. This change of colour from white to yellow takes about three weeks; the reverse takes six days. The spider sits in wait for an innocent prey on the flower, grabs it with its front legs and kills it with its venom.

Hidden Beauty

Oregonia gracilis is found in the north-western coasts of USA and Japan. It is also called the decorator crab and has a graceful appearance. Using its front legs, the crab picks up algae, sponges, wood chips and any other marine detritus. The fragments are then modified by the crab using its mouth.

▲ The goldenrod crab spider often sits on goldenrod flowers or daisies which are white or yellow in colour

▶ Sometimes a decorator crab looks like a moving rock. It camouflages itself with different items, which is why it has been given the name 'decorator'

Hearty Meals

Like all other beings, invertebrates too need to eat to survive. They have a varied diet as some prefer to eat only plants, while others are voracious carnivores. Some are even fiercer carnivores than lions, tigers and wolves. Some invertebrates are decomposers, which means that they feed on dead plants and animals. Few are omnivores, which means that they eat plants as well as animals.

Aristotle's Lantern

The common sea urchin is an omnivore. Like the name suggests, it lives in the sea and eats algae, seaweed as well as mussels and barnacles. This animal feeds by means of a complex structure called Aristotle's lantern. Five plates made of calcified materials surround the mouth and come together as a beak. The sea urchin uses this beak to scrape off algae from the rocks. Scraping causes wear and tear of the plates, but the sea urchin has the ability of growing them back. Its mouth is located on the lower part of its body, while the anus is at the top. It has got a powerful bite, strong enough to eat the toughest of seaweeds.

▲ Some species of sea urchins have venomous spines on their bodies that are harmful to human beings

The Giant Crawl

Scolopendra gigantea is the world's largest centipede, reaching the length of almost 30 centimetres. The invertebrate is found in Central America and parts of South America. All centipedes are carnivores, but these can even immobilise and hold small vertebrates such as mice, frogs, small birds and bats using their poisonous forcipules, which are venom-filled sharp claws. Apart from vertebrates, the *Scolopendra gigantea* eats insects, spiders, snails and worms.

They have 21–23 pairs of legs and spiny rear legs with which they can attack their predators. They are nocturnal creatures with poor eyesight, but their antennae help them sense the prey. *Scolopendra gigantea* have numerous spiracles or respiratory openings; due to these openings, the creatures can lose water, leading to dehydration. To avoid this fate, they live in moist areas.

▲ *Scolopendra gigantea* can refer to the Peruvian giant yellow-leg centipede or the Amazon giant centipede

▶ Dung beetles are decomposers

Dung Eaters

Dung beetles are one tough species. As the name suggests, they primarily survive on dung of animals such as cattle and sheep; however, there are also a few who eat decomposing leaves and other rotting matter. The larvae eat solid dung, while the adults suck out nutrition from the dung ball.

In Australia, the native dung beetles have been known to feed on kangaroo dung but find it difficult to decompose dung from cattle and sheep. Australia has a large number of both of these animals; hence the breakdown of their faeces became an issue. So, African and European dung beetles were introduced in Australia in order to tackle the same.

The Ancient Sponges

Sea sponges are ancient animals with a basic structure. They evolved about 500 million years ago and have outlived the dinosaurs. These simple animals live in the seas, in shallow waters as well as in the depths of the ocean, as deep as 8,500 metres. You will rarely find a floating sponge; these are seen attached to rocks, sand or mud. There are close to 5,000 species of sponges in the world.

Primitive Sponge

Sponges are animals with no organs. They have no eyes, legs, blood, heart or brain. They are made of cells and fibres, which form the outer lining, surrounding a central cavity. The most important part of the sponge is its pores. It is through these pores that water moves in and out, filtering out the food needed for its existence, removing waste materials and supplying the animal with oxygen.

Diet

Sponges eat microorganisms, seaweed, animal eggs, larvae and even small crustaceans such as barnacles and crabs.

Colourful Sponge

Sponges can range from a size of 0.5 centimetres to almost 6 feet in height. A sponge discovered in Hawaii in recent times is as large as a minivan. It is almost 12 feet long and 7 feet wide.

Some species of sponges are shapeless, while there are others with a distinct shape. Tubular or vase sponges have structures like chimneys that create air currents to suck water into their feeding chambers. Some other species, such as the sea orange, have a spherical shape, while others may be shaped like cups or fans.

Deep-water dwelling sponges have a dull appearance, while those living in shallow waters come in an array of colours ranging from violet, blue, pink, red, and yellow to even black. Few sponges appear green because of the green algae residing in them. Algae and sponges share a symbiotic relationship, which means they are mutually helpful to each other. The algae find their homes in sponges, while the sponges get nutrition from them.

◀ *These large green organisms are called brain corals. Their name is inspired by the several deep grooves on the surface that resemble the grooves in human brains*

ANIMALS | INVERTEBRATES

 ## Reproduction

To create the next generation, some sponges grow buds, which break away from the main body and grow into new sponges; while others are hermaphrodites, which means that they have both male and female germ cells in them, which are brought together to create larvae.

The larvae swim away from the primary sponge. They float around for a few hours or days, until they find an attachment, where they grow into new adult sponges. Sponges can live for a year based on the environmental conditions of their surroundings. Few are known to live for several years. Sponges could at times be attacked by disease of which not much is known.

 ## In Real Life

In ancient Greece and Rome, sponges were used to apply paint or as mops. Now they are used in surgical medicine, painting, pottery, decoration and even for bathing. The best sponges are found in the Mediterranean Sea. They have been gathered so extensively that the population has declined rapidly. It is said it will take years for it to grow back. Due to the restrictions put by governments, sponges cannot be taken from the wild anymore. They are commercially grown in various parts of the world.

▲ *Sponges are filter-feeders which means they capture microbes from the water that passes through their pores*

 ## Spikes and Pokes

Some sponges are smooth in appearance, while others have projections called spicules. These are rough, hard and sharp. They are made of substances such as lime or chalk. They don't just give firmness to the body of a sponge, but also help keep away predators.

Defence

Most sponges need saltwater to survive. However, there are a few which grow in brackish water while members of the *Spongillidae* family live in fresh waters. Sponges cannot bear to be in the open air for long. If air fills up in their pores, they wither away.

Some types of snails, slugs, crabs and fish eat sponges. Not too many animals like to make sponges their food because of their disagreeable smell as well as taste. This is why the hermit crab is smart. It makes the sponge its home. Predators such as fish stay away from these unpleasant sponges, so the crab leads a protected life.

▶ *A scuba diver comes across some tube sponges in the waters of Philippines*

The Colourful Corals

There are almost 5,000 species of corals found in the world. Like sponges, these are ancient animals, having existed for almost 500 million years. The individual organism is called a polyp, which can survive on its own, but prefers to live in colonies called coral reefs. Corals cannot grow in fresh water, so they live in the salty seas.

Coral Polyp Interior

Coral polyps are tiny animals resembling sea anemones. Their base is a hard structure made of calcium carbonate, also called limestone. It is called the calicle. This is the basic structure of a coral reef.

The coral **polyp** resembles a vase filled with flowers. The mouth of the polyp is the only opening present. It takes in food and also removes waste. It is surrounded by tubular tentacles, which are covered with nematocytes or stinging cells. These are used for defence or to sting a prey. Also, they help the mouth carry out its functions.

The polyp is covered with an outer epidermis layer and an inner gastrodermis layer. Between the two is mesoglea, a jelly-like substance, which acts as a **hydrostatic** skeleton. The stomach is made up of digestive filaments, which aid in digestion. Individual polyps are connected with one another by a small filament of living tissue called coenosarc.

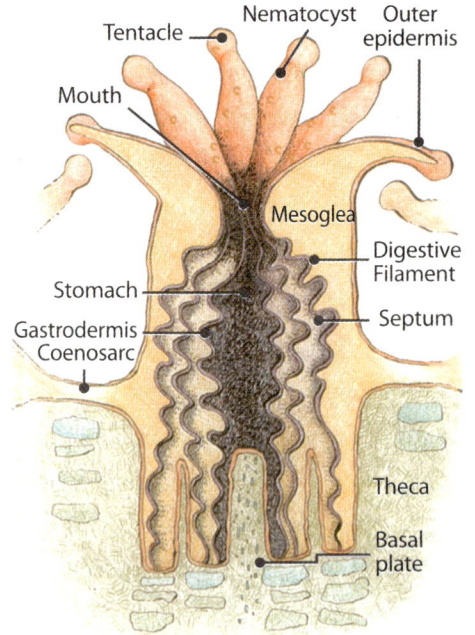

▲ The average polyp can be 1–3 millimetres in diameter

A Dash of Colour

Did you know a coral polyp is actually transparent? Then how are the reefs so colourful? Inside the coral live tiny colourful algae called zooxanthellae. They impart vibrant and colourful shades to the reefs. Corals and algae share a symbiotic relationship. While corals offer homes to the algae, algae absorb waste in the form of carbon dioxide and phosphates and provide the corals with the essential oxygen and other by-products of photosynthesis. Corals are known to eat plankton and small fish.

Beautiful Creation

Once a year, after a full moon, when the water temperature is correct, the entire colony of corals produces male and female gametes, or germ cells. It is a spectacular sight, with cascades of small, tiny specks floating in the water. The male and female gametes come together to create small larvae called planula. These larvae float in the water for a short time, before they embed themselves on rocks. If the conditions are right, a coral colony formation begins, which grows at a rate of 4 inches per year.

🛈 In Real Life

The best place in the world to see the coral reefs is the Great Barrier Reef off the coast of eastern Australia. Almost the size of Japan, it is home to innumerable species of sea turtles, whales, dolphins, sea snakes and almost 10 per cent of the world's total fish species.

▶ Due to the effects of global warming, coral reefs are dying off. Some species of corals have become threatened. Scientists are working hard to restore coral reefs using various techniques like coral farming, reattaching broken coral pieces, etc

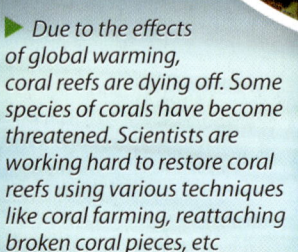

ANIMALS | INVERTEBRATES

▲ A scuba diver explores the cracks within a coral reef, assessing the damage

💡 Isn't It Amazing!

Do you know why corals are found in shallow, warm tropical waters? It is so that the Sun's rays penetrate deep enough to help algae with photosynthesis, a reaction necessary for the existence of corals. Coral reefs should remain healthy for a balanced environment.

🐾 A Complete Life

When a coral polyp dies out, a new polyp uses the remains as a base to attach itself to the reef. In this way, the reef keeps expanding, creating an ecosystem that supports more than 25 per cent of marine life. The reefs provide animals with safe places to live, hide and find food at.

Today, coral reefs are threatened by pollution and global warming. When they feel stressed due to environmental changes, they simply expel their resident algae. This is when the reef looks bleached. If the stress is not reversed, the colony starts to die out. In many parts of the world, corals are reaching this fate and sadly, it spells doom for many species that thrive in this fragile ecosystem.

Scientists are trying to reverse the effects of global warming on coral reefs by reattaching the coral pieces to coral reefs. Scuba divers are further trained to work on restoration projects. They attach new pieces of corals to the reefs using a type of cement. This gives the coral reef another chance for survival.

▼ Fish and other living species rely on coral reefs for food, shelter and protection from predators

Parasitic Invertebrates

Living inside another plant or animal can be a good source of nutrition. This is exactly what parasites do to have their needs met. A parasite lives inside a host without a symbiotic relationship. The host provides the parasite with food, water and shelter. In return, the parasite might harm the host or simply live without causing major issues.

Tapeworms

Tapeworms are flat, segmented and can parasitise the digestive tracts of many vertebrate species, including human beings. The largest of the tapeworms live in sperm whales and can grow to almost 100 feet. In human beings, tapeworms can be as long as 60 feet.

Adult Stage

An adult tapeworm living in the human gut has a head or a scolex, which attaches to the gut wall and suckers and a tail of hundreds of identical segments or proglottids. A tapeworm has no intestine and absorbs nourishment through its surface.

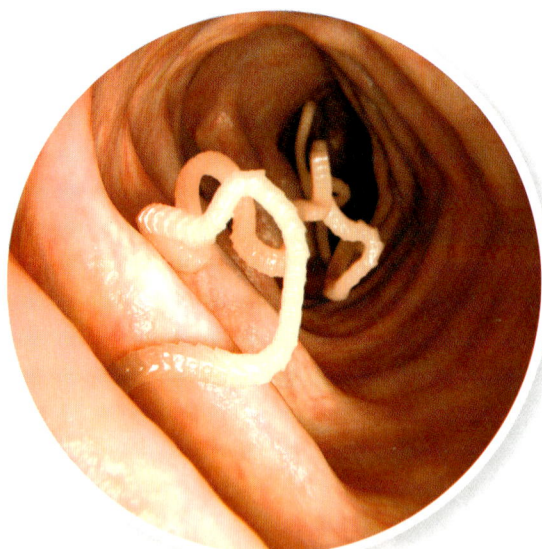

▲ Tapeworms seen in a human being's gut.

Lifecycle

Mature segments carrying tapeworm eggs break off from the tail and are excreted as faeces by the host. Many times it happens that the infected segments are eaten by cattle or pigs while taking in their food. The eggs enter the animal's intestine. Intestinal **enzymes** in the gut breakdown the eggshells. The eggs penetrate the intestinal wall and through the bloodstream are carried to the muscles where they develop into larvae. These larvae are called oncospheres.

If a human being happens to eat undercooked pig or cattle meat carrying the tapeworm, he or she is infected. The worm attaches itself to the human gut once more and the cycle is repeated. There are 54 species of tapeworms which can infect human beings.

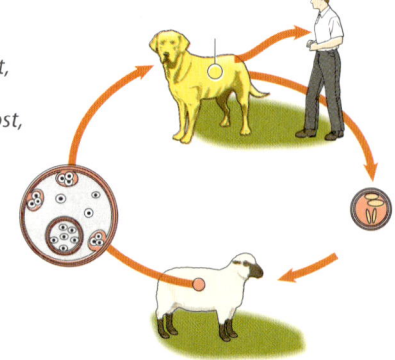

▶ The life cycle of a tapeworm with its first host, the dog and its intermediate host, the sheep.

Threat to People

Most often tapeworms cause weight loss, abdominal pain, loss of appetite, diarrhoea and weakness in human beings. In rare cases, they may lead to intestinal blockage. In this case, the doctor gives a course of medicine to clear out the infection.

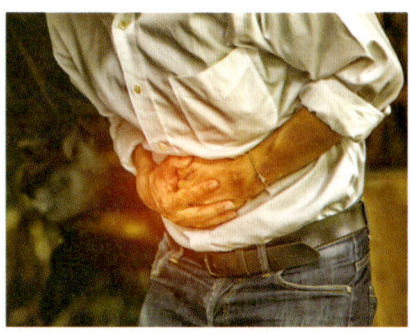

▲ A tapeworm infection in a human being can cause abdominal pain among other symptoms

★ Incredible Individuals

Before the 17th century, it was a little difficult to learn about diseases caused by tapeworms as most people could not differentiate between the various tapeworm species. By the 17th century, people knew that there were two distinct and separate types. It was Felix Plater, a physician from Switzerland, who described the two tapeworms—*Diphyllobothrium latum* and *Taenia*. Plater overcame several obstacles to complete his studies as he grew up at a time when religious persecution terrorised his country. After completing his studies, he became a physician and professor of medicine. He also studied anatomy, making several important discoveries in the field.

ANIMALS | INVERTEBRATES

A Rounded Existence

Nematodes, also known as roundworms, are one of the most abundant animals on Earth. They have a range of habitats and can live as parasites in plants, animals and human beings. They live in soil, freshwater, marine environments and even in items such as vinegar and beer. Close to 20,000 identified species exist. However, there could be more in number according to scientists. Roundworms come in a range of sizes, right from the microscopic variety to ones that are as long as 23 feet.

In Real Life

Ascaris lumbricoides is a parasitic roundworm which causes infection in human beings. The infection is common in warm tropical regions. The *ascaris lumbricoides* can grow to a size of 35 centimetres! If the host carries both male and female worms, on fertilisation, a female can lay more than 2,00,000 fertilised eggs per day.

Elephantiasis

The filarial worm, belonging to the phyla nematode, causes elephantiasis. This is an unpleasant tropical disease. The victim's affected body parts, mainly the legs, swell up to gigantic proportions. The filarial worm needs two hosts. One is the mosquito; it is in the mosquito's body that the worm completes its larval phase. Once the mosquito bites human beings, it diffuses the larvae into the human body. The larvae complete their journey to adulthood in the lymphatic system. Once here, they block the system, leading to swelling of tissues and further weaken the affected body part.

▲ *Tiny filarial worms lead to big swellings*

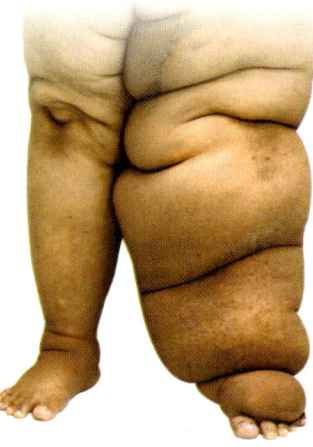
▲ *The legs of a person suffering from elephantiasis shown for comparison*

The Oak Apples

Hard, round marble galls, also called oak apples are commonly seen on oak trees. It is the tree's response to an infection caused by a parasitic insect called the gall wasp. The female lays eggs on the tissues of leaves or twigs of the oak tree. When the eggs hatch, the tissues around the larvae, also called grubs, swell up, creating gall. When the grub leaves the gall, it creates a hole. Most often, the affected twig or leaf is shed off by the tree. In general, galls do not affect the life of an oak tree, unless there are numerous ones on the bark as well.

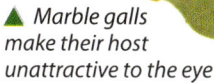
▲ *Marble galls make their host unattractive to the eye*

▶ *The gall wasps are tiny in size*

▲ *Oak apples are sponge-like and spherical in shape.*

The Slimy Snails

Phylum Mollusca is truly a diverse world consisting of more than 1,00,000 species which reside in marine, freshwater and terrestrial environments. Of these, commonly seen are snails, the slow creatures which inhabit almost all gardens in the world, especially after heavy rainfall.

Habitat

Apart from gardens, snails live in varied habitats. They live in oceans, freshwater lakes, ponds, rivers and on land. When they are on land, snails are found in dark places such as rock crevices and wood logs. Many live near water sources, as they need to keep themselves moist. This is because, like amphibians, snails have thin skin which does not retain moisture.

◀ *Next time you see a snail, remember to notice the slime it leaves behind*

Snail Trail

Have you seen a snail moving? If so, you might have noticed a trail of something wet that it leaves behind on its path. This is the slime released by the animal to move forward with minimum friction. Also, snails use their slime in harsh weather conditions, such as summers and winters. They seal the shell entrance with slime, which hardens and acts like a door that protects the animal inside. In conducive weather conditions, the slime plug is broken, and the snail moves about freely.

Protection

Snails need to protect themselves from predators. How do they do it? They have a shell made up of calcium carbonate. This protects their internal organs. The interesting feature about the shell is its spiral structure. Also, snails have an organ called the operculum. It is like a flap; the moment the invertebrate senses danger, it retreats into the shell, pulling the flap over the opening.

▲ *There are many snail species like burgundy snails, garden snails, land snails, etc*

▶ *Snail shells attached to a plant*

In Real Life

Apart from snails, oysters, clams, mussels, scallops, squids and winkles are a few molluscs eaten around the world. They are an important source of food for people living in coastal regions. The practice of snail harvesting has led to many of their species being put on the endangered list of animals.

Snail Senses

These invertebrates have four tentacles. The two lower ones are used to smell, while the two upper ones are sensory, which means they help them feel. The upper tentacles often have two eyes at the ends. These tentacles can be retracted completely.

Diet

A snail's tongue has many teeth; they are called radula and there can be thousands of them. These help snails chop through algae and plants sticking to rocks. Few larger snails are meat eaters. Snails that are decomposers are friends to human beings. They help in breaking down dead plant and animal material; and the soil regains its nutrients, making farmers happy. Snails are also used in a French delicacy called escargot, which is popular all over the world. The name literally means 'edible snail'.

▲ The shell and tentacles of a snail

Powelliphanta

Powelliphanta are large snails, with an oversized shell in a hue of colours such as red, yellow, black and brown. These snails live in the grasslands and forests of New Zealand. They are carnivores. They love earthworms in particular and also eat slugs.

Reproduction

Different snails reproduce in different ways. Some are **hermaphrodites**, which means they are male and female at the same time. Many of these snails do not need a partner to produce babies. Some snails need a partner even if they are hermaphrodites. Some other snail species have distinct male and female members.

Snails lay eggs in a clutch. These are attached to a wood log, tree or ground. In water, snail eggs attach themselves to rock surfaces. They are covered with a jelly to prevent them from drying. Each clutch can have a few to as many as 600 eggs. The Chinese mystery snail can lay almost 100 eggs, while Ramshorn snails lay only about 10–12 eggs.

Isn't It Amazing!

Most molluscs have a large and strong muscular foot. It is this foot that helps these animals move, dig, attach and capture prey. Snails are gastropods or 'stomach-footed'. They are called so because their muscular foot is on the lower part of their body, near the stomach. It is this that helps them move.

▲ The shell of the largest marine snail, the Australian trumpet, can grow to almost 2 feet in length

▲ The spike-topped apple snails are large freshwater snails from South America with a shell diameter as big as 10 centimetres

▼ The African giant snail is the largest land snail in the world with a shell that is almost 8 inches long

Meet the Squids

Squids belong to the family of the elusive cephalopods that also includes octopuses and cuttlefish. The ten-armed cephalopods are a part of the order Teuthoidea and are abundant in both coastal and ocean waters. They have short heads and long tubular bodies.

Body

The 10 arms of the squids have diverse features to help their survival. Two of these arms are slender tentacles and the rest are toothed, brisk rings that they use for suction. Their bodies are protected by a sharp internal shell. They have very distinct eyes located on the sides of their head and excellent vision. Some species of squids are swift swimmers whereas some attach themselves to plankton for movement. Squids usually eat small crabs and fish. They are eaten by whales, bony fishes and human beings.

▼ There are several species of squids in the oceans. Below is an example of the hooked squid

The Flying Squid

There have been many sightings of squids who are airborne. Scientists have always known of their gliding abilities, but numerous recent sightings indicate that some species of squids actively 'fly'. So, referring to the act as gliding may underrepresent this agile airborne quality.

▲ Japanese flying squid

These flying squids flap their fins like wings and flare their tentacles in a radial pattern, as if controlling their trajectories. Squids thrust themselves above water by a process called jet propulsion. They have a soft mantle that soaks up water. They also have a flexible tube right below their head that shoots out this water. By adjusting the direction of the tube, they determine the direction of their flight. They use this technique underwater to feast on prey and escape predators. However, in more recent times, squids have been seen using this ability to fly above water as well. Some squids also swim backwards by spreading their tentacles in a web-like fashion. Scientists have spotted squids using this technique to stop or slow down even as they fly.

Exploding Populations

Squids have fast-paced lives. They live only for a year and lay many eggs that mature rapidly. Their young have low mortality rates because their eggs are covered with a protective layer. However, scientists have tracked a change in the lifecycle of the squids because of climate change. The Humboldt squids previously weighed one to two kilograms and followed the one-year life cycle. But now they thrive in the warm waters of the eastern Pacific. The winters have been getting colder, resulting in a longer maturity cycle for these squids. They end up growing extremely large in size.

▶ A young baby squid under water. They eat small shrimp, fish and crabs

ANIMALS | INVERTEBRATES

Changing Colours

Squids are skilled at changing their colours just like chameleons and octopuses. They do it to camouflage and hide from potential predators. They can also glow brightly. Squids have two special groups of pigment cells called chromatophores and photophores present in their skin. Chromatophores are controlled by muscular contractions. By modifying the size of these cells, squids can change the colour of their bodies. They have powerful eyesight that can detect both intensity and colour of different lights. They use this feature to mirror the colour of the ocean floor or any landscape they want to blend in with.

Squids change colours in order to threaten or warn the prey as well as to hide from their predators. With the chromatophore cells, squids produce an intense light by the process of bioluminescence. This happens because of combustion between luciferin, oxygen and the enzyme luciferase. By the end of this reaction, the organism typically emits a blue-green glow. This light can be used for many functions, one of them being communication.

▲ *A glowing purpleback squid that naturally changes colour in the ocean. It also changes to a bright pink*

Elusive Giants

Giant squids are the largest ones on record. They grow to 13 metres in length. Some giant squids are 900 kilograms in weight. Though they are so huge, scientists have a hard time finding them because they live deep underwater. They are studied using their dead bodies that float to the surface.

Incredible Individuals

Tsunemi Kubodera is a zoologist from Japan. In 2004, he managed to capture a photograph of the giant squid in its natural habitat with his team. He was then able to record the giant squid on film. Both times he captured an adult and live giant squid. He also managed to film the animal in its natural habitat. He was the first to do all this, but it was not easy finding the elusive giant squid.

▲ *A specimen of the giant squid. It measures four metres, excluding its tentacles*

The Friendly Earthworms

Worms are so varied and numerous across the world that they form different groups. One such group is the annelids. Their elongated bodies are divided into numerous ring-like segments. They are found in oceans, burrowing in land or even attaching themselves to the host as blood suckers. There are about 9,000 identified species of these worms in the world today.

◀ *Earthworms live in the soil*

Habitat

Earthworms are native to Europe. However, they are found in big numbers in North America as well as western Asia. They do not live in the desert regions or areas with permanent snow coverage as such conditions do not suit them.

Burrowed Life

The annuli or the segments of the earthworm are covered with small bristles called setae, which help the earthworm move. The average length of the earthworm might be 7–9 centimetres, but it can burrow almost up to 6.5 feet deep into the soil. It can burrow all day, and crawl above to feed at night.

Diet

The mouth of the earthworm is at its first segment. They eat soil, taking in nutrients from the dead leaves and roots. A single earthworm can eat almost one-third its body weight. The remains are excreted as casts. It is the highly nutritious cast that transports minerals and other vital nutrients to the surface of the soil, making it richer for the plants growing in it. Through their burrowing, the worms aerate the soil. No wonder this small animal is a friend to the farmers.

Reproduction

Earthworms are hermaphrodites, which means a single animal will have both male and female parts. But they do not self-fertilise. They need another earthworm to create the next generation.

The main part through which the exchange of sex cells takes place is the saddle or the clitellum. It is seen as a bulge with several enlarged segments. It is through this that the earthworms exchange the sperms or the male cells to fertilise the egg cells. On mating, each worm forms a small cocoon using the liquid secreted by the clitellum. It is in this that the exchanged cells are stored. The cocoon slips off the body of the earthworm and is buried in the soil. In two to four weeks, small baby earthworms are born.

▲ *Baby earthworms pulled from the earth*

◀ *Earthworms work together to loosen the soil as they move their bodies*

The Bloodthirsty Leeches

Leeches are slightly flat-looking worms. These muscular worms can lengthen and shorten their bodies as desired. They have 34 segments on their bodies along with suckers, which distinguish them from other worms. The suckers are present at both ends—a small one at the front and a large one at the posterior end. Leeches can be small or big. The giant Amazon leech can grow almost up to 45 centimetres in length.

Quest for Survival

Some leeches prey on small worms, insect larvae and snails. The horse leech can grow up to 30 centimetres long and swallow its food whole. Other leeches are parasites. They live on the bodily fluids of other animals.

The leech clamps itself onto other animals. It then uses its three sets of tiny teeth to make its way into the skin. It sucks blood and other bodily fluids up to almost five times its weight. The giant Amazon leech uses its six-inch long proboscis as a needle to suck blood from the host. A leech can survive for weeks before needing another feed. This is because there is a pouch in its digestive system where it can store the food that it eats for weeks or even months. So, leeches do not need to find food very often.

▲ Some species are parasitic. Some eat organic waste or debris only. There is diversity within leech species

▲ The bodies of leeches are segmented. Notice the 34 segments on this leech's body

Usefulness

Leeches can suck blood from their host and make it weak. They also attach themselves to human beings. The use of leeches in therapy or treatment is called 'leech therapy'. This was very common before modern medical practices evolved. Doctors used leeches to increase blood circulation and break down blood clots.

There is a species called the European medicinal leech. It is now used to prevent blood clots in human beings during surgery. There is a substance extracted from the tissue of the leech's body called anticoagulant hirudin which is used for the purpose of preventing blood clots. Apart from this, the saliva in leeches contains substances that can anesthetise wounds. Also, substances from the Amazonian leeches are used to dissolve blood clots.

▶ In the older days, when a patient had his fingers re-attached, he might have had to use leech therapy to prevent blood build-up

In Real Life

The bright red tubifex is also called a bloodworm because of its colour. The colour is due to the presence of haemoglobin, a pigment known for its affinity to oxygen. It is the same pigment present in human beings. It takes oxygen from the water and transports it through the skin of the worm. The pigment is so abundant that the bloodworm can even stay in stagnant water with very low oxygen content. In general, these worms are found in freshwater. Some of them are also brown or tan in colour.

Crabs & Other Crustaceans

Crustaceans belong to the arthropod group. Crabs, lobsters, shrimps and prawns are common examples of crustaceans. They have tough, calcareous exoskeletons. They also have two pairs of appendages in front of the mouth and paired appendages near the mouth which function as jaws. There exist about 45,000 species of crustaceans across the world. Most of these are aquatic in nature.

Crabby Behaviour

When we talk about crustaceans, the most common one that comes to mind is the crab. Crabs are a delicacy around the world. A typical crab has a hard, shell-like cover with a small abdomen tucked inside it. It has five pairs of limbs. One pair consists of large pincers and four pairs consist of the limbs used for walking. Crabs live in sea water, but there are exceptions which live in rivers and lakes.

▲ *The stone crab can regenerate its claws if they are removed*

Out of the Blue

The blue crab has a tint of sapphire blue in its claws. This is where it gets its name from. The female blue crab has bright orange tips on her claws. Its shell is brownish in colour. It is found around coastal waters right from Nova Scotia till Uruguay. The crab is an omnivore, which means it eats both plants as well as meat. It eats mussels, smaller blue crabs, snails, fish and even carrion.

Large male crabs can have a shell width of almost 22 centimetres. These crabs are excellent swimmers because they use their paddle-shaped hind appendages to swim. They are known for their sweet meat because of which they are harvested in large numbers. Unfortunately, since they are sensitive to the environment and climatic changes, their numbers are on the decline.

Baby Boom

Blue crabs, like other hard-shelled crustaceans, mate only after the female has moulted. Yes, most crabs moult, which means they shed their exoskeleton to regrow a new one. Mating occurs when the new shell is soft. The male protects her in this exposed, vulnerable stage. The female blue crab lays eggs which she carries around with her. The eggs are held in place under the abdomen, with the help of firm bristles. In this stage, she is said to be 'in berry'.

When the eggs are ready to hatch, they are released as larvae. The transparent 'zoea', as the first baby stage is called, is about two millimetres long and feeds on plankton. 'Megalops' is the next stage, which is more crab-like. Finally, at the width of 2.5 millimetres, the young adult is completely like a mature crab. It just has to grow in size.

▶ *Female blue crab*

◀ *Male blue crab*

ANIMALS | INVERTEBRATES

Cousin of the Crab

Lobsters, like their crab cousins, are enjoyed as a delicacy, especially with butter and a squeeze of lime. These creatures live in varied habitats such as oceans, brackish waters and freshwaters. Like crabs, lobsters have five pairs of appendages. While four pairs allow them to walk around, the remaining one forms the sharp pincers used to hold and crush the prey. The four walking leg pairs are attached to the thorax, which is the middle part of the lobster's body. The abdomen in the lobster is at the rear end, like a tail.

Lobsters cannot see properly, but they have a sharp sense of smell and taste. They use their long antennae for the same. They feed on shellfish, small fish, algae and plankton.

This invertebrate is well-protected with a tough shell. The abdomen is covered with a series of plates. Lobsters are known to moult in order to grow. They can live for a long time, for almost 50 years. Their common abodes are rocks, sea grasses and self-dug holes.

Similar to crabs, female lobsters carry their eggs under their abdomen. They do so for almost a year, before releasing them as larvae. Their larvae go through a series of stages before they grow into adults.

Woodlice

Woodlice look like insects but are crustaceans. There are about 3,500 species of woodlice in the world and these are among the few crustaceans that live on land. These invertebrates have 14 legs and a thick exoskeleton. When they grow too big for the exoskeleton, they moult.

Woodlice have two antennae at the front end with which they sense their surroundings and two small outgrowths called uropods at the rear, which they need for navigation. Uropods also produce a chemical in some woodlice species. This chemical is used to ward off predators. Woodlice survive off of rotting plants, fungi and their own excretory matter. They live in dark and damp places, on walls and on decaying tree barks.

▲ *Most lobsters are nocturnal, scavenging marine animals. There are many species of lobsters, some of them are called true lobsters.*

In Real Life

Coconut crabs, also known as robber crabs, are large crustaceans. An adult can reach the width of almost 100 centimetres and can weigh up to 4 kilograms. Their meat is a delicacy. These crabs live on land and in water. Using their sharp pincers, they climb trees near the shore and can break open coconuts.

▲ *The coconut crab climbing a tree*

▲ *A close-up view of woodlice. The very first species of woodlice were marine species*

Creepy Crawlies

Spiders belong to an arthropod group called arachnids. The main feature of this group is that the animals here have 8 legs unlike crustaceans, which have 10 or more, while insects have 6 legs. Arachnids do not have wings or antennae. There are close to 80,000 species of arachnids spread across the world in a range of habitats, out of which 30,000 are spiders.

Appearance

The body of the spider is divided into two parts. The first part is the front cephalothorax, which consists of the spider's eyes, stomach, brain, glands that make poison, and mouth fangs. The second part is chelicerae or the spider's muscular jaws. It is the chelicerae that hold onto the prey while the spider injects it with poison.

Spiders cannot chew their food. Their fangs are like straws. They deliver enzymes into the prey, which make the prey mushy like a soup. Then they suck up the prey.

The spider also has leg-like pedipalps. These are not used for walking, but more as antennae to sense the objects that come in the spider's way. It needs the pedipalps to hold its prey and even spin the legendary spiderweb.

▲ *The underside of a spider has thousands of silk glands that extrude silk through spinnerets*

The back of the body is called the abdomen, which contains important internal organs. It is at the end of it that the silk-producing glands called spinnerets are present.

Spiders have a lot of hair on their legs. It is this hair which picks up vibrations and scents from the surroundings. Similar to other invertebrates, spiders have tough exoskeletons, which do not grow with them.

◀ *Xenesthis immanis is a stunning spider with a star on its back*

Silk Producers

Spiders make silk. It is this ability that sets them apart from other arthropods. They produce silk as a fluid containing a protein called fibroin. This solidifies into insoluble threads.

All spiders do not weave webs; instead many use the silk to spin protective cocoons around the eggs, to line their burrows and to create a safety line (just in case they tumble). They also make these cocoons to wrap up their prey.

Spider silk is a strong, tenacious material. It is so strong that many spiders attach their silk thread to something, like the bark of a tree and use it to swing long distances. The spider's silk comes in different forms. The cocoon silk is delicate and soft, while the silk used to spin webs is sticky.

▲ *An argiope spider building an egg case of silk after laying a yellow cluster of eggs*

Webs

To spin a web, the spider needs some support like an anchor for the web's threads. This support could be rocks, vegetation or any other solid surface. The spider selects a high perch and lets the thread travel until it touches and sticks to another object. More threads are spun, making a dense network.

Most webs are traps, but do not trap the spider itself. This is because it walks only on dry threads and uses special brushes on its claws to grip the threads. Spiders also release oil which forms a coating on their feet to prevent them from sticking to the web.

Spiderwebs could be in perfect geometric patterns or simply a mass of tangled threads. If the web is badly damaged, the spider can eat its own silk to reproduce it and make a new web.

The moment the prey touches the web, the silk wraps around it. The spiders using their fangs, release the poison. Once the prey is paralysed, it is unwrapped and consumed.

▲ Spiders have four pairs of eyes, and unlike other arthropods, have very keen vision

Poisonous Spiders

Though almost all spiders have poison, not all are harmful enough to hurt human beings. But there exist a few species of spiders with poison so powerful that they can harm most animals, including human beings. The black widow spider is a fierce arachnid, with its poison said to be deadlier than that of a rattlesnake. Its sting affects people too. If a human being is injected with the poison, they might have nausea, aches in their muscles and breathing problems. The female black widow spider, after mating, at times eats the male spider. A close cousin, the brown widow spider, has poison twice as potent, but it is less aggressive.

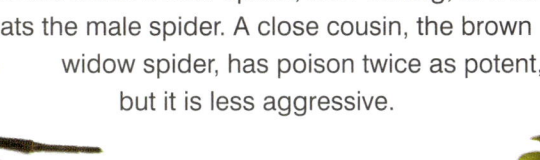

◀ Black widow spider

▶ Brazilian wandering spider

Isn't It Amazing!

The largest spider is the Goliath birdeater of South America. The body measures 12 centimetres, with a leg span of 28 centimetres. As the name suggests, it catches birds (although not very frequently), small mammals like mice, lizards and other spiders as well.

▲ The Goliath birdeater has an average weight of 170 grams

Setting a Trap

Trapdoor spiders live in burrows. Using their silk, they create a hinged door-like structure. The webbed door detects even the smallest of vibrations as a creature passes by. The silk in the web acts like a trap. Sometimes, the spider also lays long silk strands around the burrow which act like trap wires. The moment a creature touches the silk, the spider lying in wait, darts out of the burrow to inject it with its poison. It then drags the prey into the burrow, closing the trapdoor once more. Brazilian wandering spiders are considered to be the deadliest in the world. They not just use an aggressive defence position by raising their front legs in the air, but also have venom that is toxic even to the human nervous system. Their stings are said to be fatal on small children.

Star of the Show

The word echinoderm means 'hedgehog skin' in Greek and many of the species in this group are indeed spiny. These creatures live in the marine waters, so not many are familiar to us. But perhaps the most known and favourite is the starfish. In recent years the name starfish has been replaced with sea star, because the animal is technically not a fish.

Sea Stars

There are about 2,000 species of sea stars living in the warm and cold oceanic waters of the world. The most commonly known are the ones with five arms, but do you know there are species with as many as 40 arms? Underneath each arm, there are tiny tube-like feet which act as suction pumps, giving the sea star a unique adaptation that makes it capable of climbing vertical rocks. The arms have light-sensitive spots at the tips that help sea stars find food. These invertebrates have bony, spiny exoskeletons which protect them against their predators. Also, the bright colours act as a camouflage or a tool to ward off predators.

Regeneration

Sea stars have amazing regeneration skills. They can shed limbs in defence or to combat injury. The injured limb usually dies off. In its place, a new limb grows from the stump. Sometimes the new part is smaller than the original one. At other times, it branches into two, creating a six-limbed sea star.

▲ *The back and front faces of the sea star*

Hunters

Sea stars are aggressive hunters. They feed on molluscs such as clams, mussels, oysters and snails. They have an interesting technique to hunt down bivalve molluscs such as mussels. They grip the shell of mussels or similar creatures with their strong tube feet and keep pulling until the bivalve is exhausted and its shell opens.

Diet

A sea star spills its stomach into the mouth of the prey. Enzymes from the sea star digest the prey, after which it is ingested by the animal. The stomach returns to its original place.

Crown-of-thorns Starfish

The crown-of-thorns starfish is an interesting invertebrate. Its arms number up to 21 with hundreds that are 4 centimetres in length. They are toxin-filled thorns. This sea star is a bane to the coral reefs. It can eat almost 10 square metres of coral reefs in one year. Also, a single female can produce close to 50 million eggs in one year. Australian coral reefs have suffered many an outbreak of crown-of-thorns, leading to massive destruction. Outbreaks of these starfish on coral reefs are often the result of overfishing, where the natural predator of the crown-of thorns starfish is removed.

◀ *A close view of the crown-of-thorns starfish*

Breakaway

Brittle stars are cousins of the sea stars. They have close to 2,100 living species in the group. As the name suggests, the brittle star is indeed brittle. Parts of its long, delicate arms break off to regenerate soon. It has five arms radiating from a central disc. These arms can grow almost up to 2 feet in larger species. It uses its flexible arms to crawl across the sea floors.

Most brittle stars do not prefer the shallow tidal waters. They are found in deeper waters. Sometimes hundreds of brittle stars are found piled up on the sea floor. They feed on plankton, worms and small molluscs. They also feed on the detritus, thus making them scavengers.

▶ The brittle star is also called serpent star

 ## Like Feathers

Feather stars are also cousins of the sea star. They have 550 existing species. These invertebrates have feathery arms, which are used both for swimming and feeding. They use their legs called cirri to settle on corals, sponges or any other perch in the sea. They move their long arms to capture edible material floating in water. Feather stars are commonly found in waters of the Indian Ocean right up to Japan.

 ## Like the Lily

Similar to its namesake, the flower lily, sea lilies have a long stalk with which they attach themselves to the ocean. They have feathery arms that sway in the water. They may resemble a flower but are actually echinoderms. Most live in deep waters of the ocean, along the sea beds. They live on detritus or floating edible particles. Other starfish also resemble the sea lily but they do not have the stalk, thus allowing them to be much more mobile than sea lilies.

▶ Feather stars and sea lilies may look like plants, but they are related to starfish. All of them are echinoderms

Word Check

Cephalisation: It refers to the presence of sense organs and brain in the upper part of the body.

Chitinous: It refers to animals with a semi-transparent substance which forms part of the exoskeleton in arthropods.

Coelom: It is the fluid-filled body cavity which acts as a cushion for the internal organs.

Enzymes: They are substances produced by living organisms which bring about a biochemical reaction.

Hermaphrodites: It means an organism has both male and female sex organs.

Hydrostatic: It is associated with fluids and their pressure.

Myriapods: It is an arthropod group; the animals have elongated bodies with numerous legs.

Pentamerous: It means that the parts of the body are arranged in a group of five.

Photosynthesis: It is the process by which green plants prepare food in the presence of sunlight and a pigment called chlorophyll that is present in the leaves of plants. The plants also need carbon dioxide and water to release energy and oxygen.

Polyp: It is an individual coral organism.

Single-celled bacteria: This bacteria has only one functional and structural unit.

Thorax: It is the middle section in an insect, between the head and abdomen.

Visceral: It refers to the internal organs, especially in the abdominal region.